Your Greatness Is Growing

Nurturing the Heart of Autism

Catherine Stafford, LCSW

Catherine Stafford lives with her husband and four children outside of Seattle, Washington. She is a Licensed Clinical Social Worker (LCSW) and is a certified Nurtured Heart Approach™ specialist. Contact the author directly for speaking, coaching or counseling services at www.nurturemyheart.com.

Other books by this author:
• Nurture My Heart—Igniting The Greatness In Every Child
• Teacher, Nurture My Heart—Igniting The Greatness In Every Student

Your Greatness Is Growing: Nurturing The Heart of Autism
Catherine Stafford, LCSW

Original artwork from children as noted and used with permission.

ISBN 978-0-9838610-0-3
Publisher: Greatness Grows Publications, Snohomish, Wa.

Printed in the United States of America.

Advance Reviews

"Catherine Stafford has provided parents and professionals with a rare and much needed tool—a book for kids with autism spectrum disorder (ASD) that is positive and affirming. This delightful book, and its illustrations created by kids on the spectrum, will no doubt serve to build self-esteem and support a positive sense of self for these very brave children who are faced with so many challenges in their lives." **- Barry M. Prizant**, Ph.D., CCC-SLP, director of Childhood Communication Services, and adjunct professor at the Center for the Study of Human Development at Brown University, Providence, R.I.

"Extraordinary! Stunning! Brilliant! Hopeful! This book goes beyond celebrating differences. It provides a framework for helping children navigate their everyday worlds and offers a language for celebrating successful choices. Stafford has masterfully crafted a way for children to connect the dots between behavior and emotions and takes us on a journey of seeing each moment through a different lens. This book is a MUST for all parents and caregivers of children with ASD. It honors the child from the place of the heart and provides irrefutable evidence of that child's greatness in each and every choice. It will surely be a staple on my bookshelf as ALL children thrive when they are able to tap into the core of who they are and fully embrace their gifts and qualities." **- Lisa Bravo**, MC, LPC, LISAC, NCC, psychotherapist, parenting expert and top-selling author, Chandler, Az.

"I've worked for more than a decade with several thousand families of autistic children and I'm always open to new ways of helping them. Since finding the Nurtured Heart Approach, I have referred many families to work with Catherine Stafford in applying Nurtured Heart concepts to parenting. Children of all ages and all levels of function have much to gain through Nurtured Heart parenting. Thank you for your contribution Catherine. Our greatness is growing." **- John A. Green III**, M.D., physician at EverGreen Center PC, Oregon City, Or. / Allergy, and Environmental Medicine, Childhood Disorders

"This book is not only so sweet, it is extremely comprehensive in presenting essential aspects of The Nurtured Heart Approach. The strategies have been given life in the rhyme and rhythm of Catherine's words. The children's drawings vibrantly represent the language of the approach; they are poignant and filled with the vitality of this work. By including specific references to what is going right, what could be going wrong, and using repetitive affirmations, methods proven particularly effective for autistic children are exemplified with the intentionality that positively impacts all types of children. EXCELLENT work, Catherine! Thank you!!" **- Angela R. Smith**, CAS, NCC, LPC, a Nurtured Heart counselor and coach, Hampton, Va.

"Catherine embodies the Nurtured Heart Approach. I love the positive aspect of NHA. It has helped my son with his behavior and anxiety, and he loves to talk about his greatness." **- Eileen Cooper**, parent, Everett, Wa.

"**W**ho doesn't enjoy hearing that they handled a situation well, used self-control when it was needed, or refused to let something ruin their day? Ms. Stafford's book highlights appropriate (really, excellent!) choices children make every day that most adults ignore. Then she goes further by putting a name on those choices (e.g., "responsible," "respectful," "being positive") and clearly acknowledging the child for making the choice, providing the child with evidence that, indeed, his greatness is growing. What a gift to give a child! This book should be in the office of every pediatrician, school counselor, dentist (this list could be long!) and in the home and classroom of every child who doesn't know absolutely for sure that his greatness is showing!" **- Nancy W. Kling**, owner of Behavior Plus, Inc., Friendswood, Tx.

"**C**atherine Stafford's "Your Greatness Is Growing" is a game changer! A practical road map to Nurtured Heart Approach, her latest book shows how to be your POSITIVE happy self instead of the "policewoman." Now my child and I are free to celebrate our greatest, happiest, most confident selves. Instead of a boring sermon telling him what he did wrong and why it was wrong, we literally sing and dance about our success in the moment. It's way more fun for both of us!

"Your Greatness Is Growing" keeps parents and children in the moment—as opposed to several beats behind the "moment," which is the best most of us can do without the practical advice and management skills found in "Your Greatness Is Growing."

Catherine's book guides me to anticipate, create and celebrate the daily positive moments that enable me to give my child what he needs in a simple and effective way. Before reading the book, I was exhausted! After reading "Your Greatness Is Growing," I'm simply reflecting the successful moment as it happens, thereby creating an entire day of success. It seems so simple and obvious after the fact, but Nurtured Heart Approach is counterintuitive to the way many of us were raised and, therefore, very confusing until you read the book and take the leap of faith until the light bulb goes off!

Before reading the book, I was afraid to acknowledge how proud I was that he was playing on his own because I didn't want him to stop. Acknowledging it did not stop him but rather made us both feel more connected and kept him happily playing longer. I would not have believed it had I not experienced it firsthand.

Following this simple and beautifully illustrated book makes me feel so much closer to my child and calmer—but also energized! And he's happier, too! By following the book, I get to see that twinkle in his eye all day long—and we both get to know we are celebrating our greatness. It's our little secret and what I've started referring to as our "extraordinarily ordinary" greatness!" **- Rebecca Whittington**, marketing/media consultant, film producer and parent, San Antonio, Tx.

"Your Greatness Is Growing" is dedicated to ...

the children and families of Lynnwood Speech and Language Services and Stafford Counseling Services in Lynnwood, Washington. Their greatness is reflected in every beautiful image and quote. I am indebted to Susan Stewart and Susan McLeod for their encouragement, editing and enthusiastic support; Howard Glasser for his inspiration; and Brian Stafford for believing in me. I wish to thank Mark Kunzelmann for his artistic eye and creative design. Most of all I wish to thank the children who have allowed me the joyous opportunity to walk alongside them and watch as they learn to live in greatness. It is my honor. To your greatness!

In memory of my mom, for leading the way.

- Catherine Stafford

Foreword

by Susan E. Stewart, MS, CCC-SLP

The Nurtured Heart Approach is an easy-to-implement model of interacting with children on the autism spectrum that creates profound, positive changes within the children and their families.

It is a method of engaging a child with autism in ways that facilitate the ability to regulate emotions and develop communication skills. It instills in the child a growing sense of greatness and creates a strong relationship between the child and parent, caregiver or professional. I have seen parents' relief when they realize how easy it is to shift into commenting about their child's actions and then the joy when their child engages so naturally. "Is it this easy? My child is smiling with me!"

Autism is a broad spectrum developmental disorder encompassing behavior, social communication and language, where a child can have strengths in one area and relative weakness in another. Current research demonstrates that early and continued intervention targeting the core deficits facilitates significant growth across all areas of development.

To get a better sense of how the Nurtured Heart Approach supports families and children with autism, it is important to pull from the past to better understand current philosophies on best practice. The Russian psychologist Leo Vygotsky researched how a child's knowledge and understanding of the world develops through social interactions with others who provide varying levels of support to ensure successful learning. Many notable researchers in child development and autism spectrum disorders have expanded on this early work. The combined research and contributions by T. Berry Brazelton, Stanley Greenspan (Floortime) and Barry Prizant (SCERTS) all support his theory that children require positive and shared social interaction with nurturing adults to thrive physically, socially and emotionally. The Nurtured Heart Approach also teaches adults how to develop a shared engagement by simply commenting on what is going right in the present moment—a positive reflection that communicates, "I see what you are doing and feeling. I see you being successful."

One of the primary stances of the Nurtured Heart Approach is to energize all positive behavior, with incremental movement in the right direction hailed as a victory. We often hear how children with ASD have difficulties regulating emotions. The resulting behaviors and how to extinguish them are a constant point of discussion. While this dysregulation represents the child's difficulty understanding, integrating and communicating the sensory input that he/she is receiving, it obviously interferes with a child's ability to learn and can negatively impact a family or classroom's ability to function cohesively. When the focus is on

communication grow, the child begins to define himself/herself in terms of greatness. The parents express their thrill at being able to help their children navigate through a world that can be confusing and overwhelming.

Our role as parents, caregivers and professionals is to observe and interpret the environment for a child, to remain flexible and calm, to follow a child's lead or areas of interest, and to predict and modify the environment to help maintain emotional regulation. The Nurtured Heart Approach provides parents and

I have seen parents' relief when they realize how easy it is to shift into commenting about their child's actions and then the joy when their child engages so naturally. "Is it this easy? My child is smiling with me!"

trying to extinguish a behavior or constantly putting energy into the challenging behavior, we lose the opportunity to recognize and enhance all of the behaviors that a child is displaying that promote positive interactions. It is much more powerful to teach a concept through energizing when it is being demonstrated than reprimanding or teaching out of context. As a parent learns to respond to the intent behind a behavior, the child better regulates his/her behavior. The stress decreases because the moment is seen as a time to teach instead of a behavior that is unacceptable. As emotional regulation and functional and meaningful social

professionals with tools to energize the child, as well as themselves, in a manner that promotes healthy, positive and reciprocal interactions. This paves the way for a child to more readily learn and move to higher levels of development.

It is fundamental to the success of every human being to love and to learn in environments that are safe, supportive and nurturing. The Nurtured Heart Approach creates such an environment and, thereby, creates success for families with children on the autism spectrum.

- Susan E. Stewart, MS, CCC-SLP, speech language pathologist

Introduction

by Howard Glasser, MA

For many years, I have been concerned about the burgeoning number of children diagnosed with disorders along the autism spectrum.

Conventional thinking is that these children are predominantly unavailable to positivity—both hearing it and growing deeply in positivity.

In contrast, my experience with autistic children is profoundly encouraging. I have found these children to be longing to hear the voice of their greatness, and I have seen that voice echo beautifully in their hearts and souls.

Catherine Stafford has very much become that voice.

She too, experiences that we can indeed speak to the greatness of children with autism. Catherine is taking that endeavor to an even more inspiring level than I had ever imagined possible, with amazing results.

Our culture defines greatness as something lofty that very few people can actually achieve. However, I believe that greatness is in the heart and soul of every single child—that it's in our "soulware."

Catherine proves this is infinitely true for the child with autism, and she has created a road map for parents and teachers that lights up the runway so that they can get this greatness-igniting process under way as well.

Let me give you a little prelude to understanding the nature of the Nurtured Heart Approach, and she will take you the rest of the way.

We often view behavior and character in children in terms of what is expected versus what is undesired.

Expected behavior and good character get very little recognition—at best, the low-energy and relationship of "thank you" and "good job." Conversely, undesired behaviors are recognized with big emotional energy and juicy relationship.

As a result, some children wind up believing there is more "high-speed connection" in terms of adult interest for misbehavior; which they essentially translate energetically as feeling more loved when they make a poor choice than a good one.

The great news is that not only can this be turned around to benefit children, but it can be turned all the way on to greatness!

When we redefine greatness as something that is inherent in each of us, something that is our birthright, and something that, unfortunately, life's nuances cover over and life's experiences chip away at, we can then seek to uncover and recover our own greatness and the greatness in our children.

Everyday actions can be transformed into greatness by how we choose to see them. It's a simple choice to honor what is good and positive that we see happening in front of us, moment by moment.

What we call out in our children (accuse them of) will magnify and grow before our eyes. When we choose to see greatness, we grow greatness. When children begin to feel greatness, they act from this place of greatness. Their internal portfolio shifts from one defined by deficits and weaknesses to one defined by growing greatness.

It's like throwing a pebble in the pond and watching the ripples just grow and grow. When children "stand in their greatness," they own it and it becomes how they define themselves—who they are to their very core.

When we honor the greatness in our children, we grow our own greatness and we become the parent that we were designed to be. As I am fond of saying, parenting then becomes a much more inspiring journey for all.

When we honor our child's greatness, we search in every moment to find and to celebrate success. We don't wait to capture them doing something wonderful, profound or above and beyond. We celebrate every purposeful step along that journey. Each step is a part of that child's greatness, and to honor their efforts in this journey provides further momentum to propel them forward with renewed zeal and enthusiasm.

You shall soon see, by the way of Catherine's magnificent guidance in "Your Greatness Is Growing," that greatness is in each and every one of us—and it's not only there for the taking, it's there for the making. Catherine shows you how.

Catherine's resolve has become the new voice of autism, and so many children now will be greatly impacted by these words. On a heart and soul level, these children will respond to what you read to them by way of the words in this book and all that is inspired by this message beyond the reading of this book.

As the creator of the Nurtured Heart Approach, I am delighted that Catherine has devoted herself to unfolding and furthering my work through her heart-warming children's books. Enjoy the journey!

- Howard Glasser, MA, creator of the Nurtured Heart Approach, founder of the Children's Success Foundation, and author of "*All Children Flourishing,*" "*Transforming the Difficult Child*" *and* "*Notching Up the Nurtured Heart Approach for Educators*", www.difficultchild.com

Letter to Parents
from the Author

"Your Greatness Is Growing" is a reflection of a child's day, in Nurtured Heart Approach fashion. This book demonstrates how everyday moments can be transformed through our language, energy and focused presence to create a string of irrefutable moments of success that no child can deny.

As a therapist, it saddened me to see that children in my office were universally unable to articulate anything good and wonderful about themselves. A request as seemingly simple as, "Tell me something that makes you proud to be you," was often met with a glassy-eyed stare or reference to some sort of external accomplishment, but never an internalized quality of that child's greatness.

How many children regularly hear about their good choices with detailed specificity and in the present moment—the ways they have been a good friend, shown great character, honored family values and managed strong feelings well? The Nurtured Heart Approach provides a clear conceptual framework that places an adult in the position to nurture everyday moments into clear successes in a child's heart and soul.

The beauty of the Nurtured Heart Approach lies in its simplicity. When you relentlessly pursue success, refuse to be drawn into or energize negativity and provide clarity with expectations, children transform themselves right before your eyes, not in a way that is transient and superficial, but deeply altering what they believe about themselves at their very core. It is about staying present in relationship, with a clear intention of creating success. The Nurtured Heart Approach is not about unfounded, over-the-top "praise," but rather refusing to miss or overlook opportunities to finesse and call out the very behaviors and character we wish to grow in our children. It is about growing greatness.

What I've seen with my clients is nothing short of miraculous. Language improves, and challenging behaviors fade simply through sending the message, "You are successful. Here you are doing it, and I'm telling you what I see. Do you see it and feel it? This is You."

Incremental movement in the right direction is hailed as victory. Frustrations and anger are turned around as kids feel experientially when they are handling their strong emotions. Limits are made clear, and all children are held to high standards of behavior. As Howard Glasser says, "We create what we see." The successes we call out in our children grow before our eyes. Choose to see the greatness; choose to grow greatness.

When I now ask the children I see about their greatness, they have answers of internalized success, an awareness of their own growing greatness. Families are less stressed, as they have shifted into deeply positive relationships and confidence in their parenting.

The Nurtured Heart Approach works to build the inner wealth of children on the spectrum. Skills and competencies, positive effort and strong character begin to be internalized in a way that is powerfully real for the child. This all happens in the context of an exceptionally positive relationship. Once the language of success is established, behaviors transform as skills are taught contextually and a new trajectory of greatness begins. We move beyond the goal of improvement to see children flourish.

This book was born in my heart as a strong and persistent, almost nagging, reminder of the qualities of greatness that all wonderful children have within them. Every child. Your child. They all deserve to hear the message of their growing greatness. It is my desire that this story will resonate with you and your child and begin your journey into greatness.

- Catherine Stafford
www.NurtureMyHeart.com
www.NHAAutismResearch.net

"I am caring and try to make others feel better when they are sad." Katie, age 7

Another fresh start, it's a brand new day.

You're growing greatness in so many ways.

Your greatness is growing; it may feel so brand new.

But it's not hard to see that this greatness is you.

This greatness is yours, with a good day or bad.

It won't go away if you're grouchy or sad.

Your greatness has been there right from the start.

It begins in your head, and it grows in your heart.

There are so many ways that your greatness will grow. How many ways, you might ask? Look at your day, and you'll know.

You showed off your greatness with all of your might, from dawn until dusk, did so many things right.

"My greatness is that I help little kids." Neomi, age 7

There are so many ways that your greatness is growing, so many ways that it's greatness you're showing.

You got up out of bed and got ready for school.

That's managing time, and it's a greatness tool.

You didn't dawdle or refuse to get dressed.

You chose to get ready, and our day was not stressed.

You could have lost track and got back into bed,

covered your head, then pretend to play dead.

But you kept on moving, getting ready for school.

You chose success, and your choice was so cool.

You're growing greatness.

"My greatness is caring about the earth."   Jackson, age 9

You go with the flow without getting upset. That's flexibility growing, and it's greatness, you bet!

You may have been angry when I changed your snack,

but you took a deep breath and then you bounced back.

You could have stayed angry, let it ruin your day.

Instead you kept it small, and the issue faded away.

That's showing greatness.

"Greatness is that I brush my teeth the first time daddy asks." Sarah, age 4

When you rode on the bus, you stayed in your seat. You had self-control, and that was no small feat.

You didn't get up and move around the school bus.

The driver was so happy, and she made such a fuss ...

About greatness.

It's not easy to sit on that long, slow bus ride.

You resisted the impulses growing inside ...

To move around that big bus, be disruptive and loud.

Your success on that bus should make you feel proud.

You're growing greatness.

"I comfort people when they are sad." Spencer, age 12

Your teacher is showing you ways that you're kind. It takes lots of effort from your powerful mind.

When you play with another and do what they like to do, you're being a friend to that kid, it's so true.

And when a student fell down on the playground at school, the other kids laughed because they don't know the rule.

But you chose to go over and to help that kid stand. That shows you have empathy, giving a hand.

You could have laughed, too, and just walked away, but your kindness was powerful proof on this day ...

You're full of greatness.

"Greatness is that I love my family, and I love being good." Alyssa, age 4

When your teacher asked questions, you raised your hand. You waited your turn, didn't get up and stand.

You could have called out, shouted loudly, "Pick me,"

but you showed self-control by waiting patiently.

You're thinking of others when you wait and don't shout.

Self-control is important—it's your greatness, no doubt.

More of your greatness.

SEATTLE MARINERS LOGO

1993—

"I have greatness." Caleb, age 8

If your friend sits too close

or the room is too loud, and you ask

just to leave and get out of that crowd ...

That was greatness.

You know what you needed and to ask was just right.

You didn't get angry and then start a fight.

You did what you could to feel calmer inside.

You handled it well and that's a huge stride ...

In your greatness.

"My greatness is that I am kindly." Taylor, age 11

Your greatness is growing, each and

every new day. Your greatness is real, it is yours and it stays.

You don't lose your greatness when you take a time out,

when you don't want to listen and impulse says to shout.

It's yours even then, when not doing your best.

Just think of this time as a small greatness test ...

And then go back to greatness.

"Greatness is that I love myself, and I love you." Christopher, age 5

When you handle uncomfortable, strong

feelings well, feel proud of yourself, let the greatness just swell.

Some feelings are hard, sometimes they feel bad,

but all feelings are yours, whether happy or sad.

All your feelings are needed, they help make you, you.

To be in touch with your feelings is just telling you ...

You're full of greatness.

"My greatness is that I go potty in the potty." Sam, age 4

You don't like loud sounds,

like the toilet when flushing, and your
heart starts to race and your energy's rushing.

But you took three steps into the bathroom today.
That's growing greatness in a most powerful way.

Some worries aren't true, but they feel scary and real.
When you challenge your worries in stages you'll feel ...

Full of greatness.

Elliot, age 8

You said, "Worries go, you get no time today.

I'm taking control of my feelings this way."

Then you challenged the worries, used logic to show,

that the worries aren't real, and it's time that they go.

That's such greatness.

"Thinking about what others are thinking." Parker, age 7

If you're playing a game

and the rules you don't bend,

then you're following rules, and you're being a friend.

It's hard not to cheat when you don't want to lose,

but sportsmanship shows that it's greatness you choose.

When playing with a friend, you kept it so real.

You were tempted to talk about the stories you feel.

These stories can keep you from joining, you see,

when you focused on him that was greatness full speed ...

So much greatness.

"I am a good friend." Alex, age 5

Then you had to be last when you hoped
to be first. To go last made you mad, you thought last was the worst.

You took three deep breaths, "Smell flowers, blow candle,"
and you knew that the issue was one you could handle.

Order's not important when playing a game.
To go last, middle, first—the fun is the same.

To know that is greatness when you play with a friend.
To show that is a powerful message to send ...

One of greatness.

"My greatness is that I mostly listen to my mom and dad right away." Nicholas, age 6

And when you don't

want to leave because you're playing a game,

but you get up and go, and your mood is still tame ...

That's also greatness.

It's so hard to stop when you want to keep going.

To stop when you're asked is greatness you're showing.

You're growing greatness.

"No matter what happens, you always have greatness." James, age 8

That greatness is you, it can't go away.
Your greatness gets bigger each and every new day.

How big can it get? Can it get bigger yet? Is there a max to your greatness?
Is the size already set? No. There's no end to greatness. Be whatever
you dream. Greatness stays with you when you're mad or you scream.

We all have hard moments when we just want to shout,

stand up on our chair or sit down with a pout.

Just "reset" to greatness, that's all you need do.

Just take a calm breath for a moment or two.

Sometimes it might take just a little bit longer;

or help from a grownup to make you feel stronger.

Just keep growing greatness.

"I am great at making friends." Kate, age 5 ½

When you make the right

choices because they are right, and no one

is watching, no reward is in sight ...

That's your greatness.

To do the right thing without getting a prize

shows your greatness is growing to remarkable size.

And when you make choices poorly, it's just a mistake.

Just do a "reset," and do a retake.

That's also greatness.

"Greatness is like a fire burning." Nathan, age 9

Your greatness is growing,

it's been growing all day. You've increased

your own greatness in some powerful ways.

You've shown it all day, it's been there from the start.

It begins in your head, and it grows in your heart.

Do you hear all the ways that your greatness is growing?

Can you feel all the ways, it's greatness you're showing?

Sean   Mom   Sean   Dad

THE COOKING CHANNEL

BOX

Sean, Age 12

"I feel great to write my 6th grade homework." Sean, age 12

At the end of the day,

when you come home from school, and now you
have homework, but you still keep your cool ...

You're showing greatness.

It's hard to stay focused when you'd rather go play,
not do more of the work you've been doing all day.

But you let someone sit, took the help that you need.
You listened to them, that was greatness indeed ...

More of your greatness.

"Greatness is sharing love with other people." Nathan, age 12

You played with your brother,

and you chose not to fight.

When he took your toy, it took all of your might ...

To choose greatness.

You stayed there with him, let him show you what to do.

You played the game his way, because he's just two.

That was greatness.

It's hard not to lead, play the game just your way.

But you taught your brother in a big brother way ...

About greatness.

"I have greatness because I am comfortable with this conversation." Andrew, age 5

We had your least favorite

dinner, but you didn't stomp your feet.

You stayed in control and didn't yell for a treat.

You ate what was served and that showed that you care.

It was such a calm meal that we all stopped and stared ...

At your greatness.

We each took turns talking about parts of our day;

you sat and listened, you didn't let your nerves fray.

You could have just left, but you chose to stay,

that was your greatness being displayed ...

Such sweet greatness.

"Everyone has greatness." Liam, age 8

Believe in your greatness!

There's so much more in store. When you feel

full of greatness, make room for some more.

Keep working on greatness each and every new day.

But know that your greatness is yours, and it stays.

No one can take it; it's yours from the start.

It begins in your head and it grows in your heart.

It's not really growing like a plant or a tree.

It's not really growing in a way that you see.

Can you feel your greatness?

"I am very strong." Cody, age 5

greatness is not whether you got that "B."

That's a product of greatness, but it goes deeper to me.

It's about what it took, to make that good grade.

It's the effort involved, and the choices you made.

You had to stay focused, know the steps of the task,

follow through to the end, and do what you were asked.

A grade's just a measure of some things that you know;

there's much more to greatness than a report card can show.

So much greatness.

"My greatness is that I am caring for animals." Anna, age 9

When the night has come, and you crawl into bed, and you want me to stay, and I leave you instead.

It's you being brave and going to sleep,

thinking calm thoughts or just counting sheep.

You could have kept asking for more books to be read,

but you didn't get up, you stayed right in your bed.

You're growing greatness.

"Being nice to John John." Gabby, age 11

You're brave and you're gentle, you're smart and you're kind,

a flexible thinker with a quickness of mind.

You're patient and calm, and you listen to rules,

you go with the flow, use your greatness tools.

Hear all the ways that it's greatness you're showing?

Can you feel all the ways that your greatness is growing?

Just wake with this thought each and every new day,

"I'm growing greatness in so many ways!"

"Greatness is that I always have courage." Gracia, age 9

Your greatness is growing

in so many ways. Your greatness is yours, it is real and it stays.

So own all of this greatness, take it into your heart.

This greatness is yours; it's been there from the start.

There are so many ways your greatness is showing,

know without doubt that your greatness keeps growing.

You're so full of greatness!

Greatness-Growing Vocabulary

Reflect on a child's greatness in each opportunity-filled moment.
Rather than "thank you" or "good job," choose to create meaningful and contextual moments
of success by accusing a child, in the moment, of being the greatness quality of ...

Being joyful   Considerate   Attentive   Cooperative   A hard worker   A source of strength

Courageous   A leader   Constructive   A helper   Committed   Creative   A great example   Courteous

An advocate   Aware   Dedicated to success   Diligent   Discerning   Direct   Accomplishing a lot

Acting creatively   Dignified   Appreciative   Easy to like   Deeply understanding   A good friend

Attentive to detail   Productive   Demonstrating integrity   Exceeding expectations   Gentle

Being inspiring   Being surprising   Efficient   Empathetic   Being powerful   Being wise   Faithful

Brave   Focused   Bringing out the best in others   Forgiving   Generous   Choosing what's important

Compassionate   Gracious   Going above and beyond   Humble   Honest   Peacekeeper   Genuine

Glorious   Productive   Good-hearted   Reasonable   Respectful   Having unique ideas   Resourceful

Energetic   Responsible   Respecting self   Reliable   Enthusiastic   Having great curiosity

Thankful   Self-controlled   Handling strong emotions well   Inspiring   Seeing the big picture

Having an open mind   Honorable   Having a positive attitude   Strong on the inside   Hopeful

Trustworthy   Independent   Thoughtful   Inquisitive   Understanding   Intelligent   Just and fair

Kind   Loving   Using a pleasant voice   Using your great mind   Vibrant   Visionary

Looking out for others   Managing time well   A quick mind   Making great choices

Brilliant thoughts   Making a great guess   Organized   Patient   A great sense of humor

A great sense of logic   Pulling together   Amazing forethought   Enthusiastic   Excellent planning skills

Great teamwork   Modest   Tenacious   Responsible   Deliberate   Showing character   Growing greatness

Draw Or Write About Your Own Greatness

CPSIA information can be obtained
at www.ICGtesting.com
Printed in the USA
270311LV00002B